# TABLE OF CONTENTS

Earth's atmosphere is made mostly of nitrogen and oxygen. It also contains gases that act like the glass panels of a greenhouse.

These "greenhouse" gases help trap heat that keeps the earth warm and able to support life.

GREENHOUSE GASES:

WATER VAPOR
CARBON DIOXIDE
NITROUS OXIDE
METHANE

INCREASE IN CARBON DIOXIDE LEVELS IN THE PAST 50 YEARS

But you can have too much of a good thing. The world is getting warmer due to increased amounts of greenhouse gases in the atmosphere.

The rise in the average temperature of earth's atmosphere is called global warming.

This warming may lead to serious problems worldwide.

But the amount of some gases, especially carbon dioxide, has been rising. More greenhouse gases mean more heat is being radiated back to earth. The result is a warmer planet.

RADIATED HEAT

Scientists believe human activities are the reason there's more carbon dioxide in the air.

HYBRID

Car exhaust, for example, contains carbon dioxide. One hundred years ago, very few cars traveled our roads.

Today, they clog our highways and release tons of carbon dioxide into the air every day.

And don't forget that breathing adds carbon dioxide to the air too. Animals and people release carbon dioxide when they exhale.

Luckily, plants help clean the air. They use carbon dioxide to make food in a process called photosynthesis.

When plants make food by taking up carbon dioxide, they release oxygen, which all animals need to live.

OXYGEN

CARBON DIOXIDE

Plants are more important than we might think, Max.

You should take a closer look at their impact on global warming.

I think I will!

Trees, plants, and even the oceans help take up extra carbon dioxide from the atmosphere.

But in many places, such as the rain forests of South America, people are clearing the forests for farmland.

**DEFINITION**

deforestation (di-for-uh-STAY-shuhn) the clearing of forests by cutting or burning trees

Trees that are burned or left to decompose release carbon dioxide into the air.

Because these dead trees no longer take in carbon dioxide, the buildup of greenhouse gases increases.

Experts use computer programs to predict how extra greenhouse gases may change the earth in the future.

They predict the average global temperature will rise 2 to 10 degrees Fahrenheit, or 1.1 to 5.6 degrees Celsius, by 2100. This warming could lead to major changes for the planet.

For example, scientists worry about what global warming will do to earth's weather and climate.

Weather describes the current state of the atmosphere, such as sunny and warm . . .

. . . or cold, rainy, and windy.

DRY CLIMATE

Climate describes the average weather of a certain area over many years.

TROPICAL CLIMATE

TEMPERATE CLIMATE

POLAR CLIMATE

Florida is normally warm and humid, for example.

And Antarctica is cold and dry.

Climates change over time, but global warming is changing them faster than normal.

13

Global warming may also change rainfall patterns, which can lead to devastating floods . . .

KLIK!

. . . and harsh droughts.

KLIK!

I need to see the effect of these higher temperatures around the world.

If you want to see how fast things are changing, you should look at glaciers.

RECORD HURRICANES

ACCESS GRANTED: MAX AXIOM

The 2005 Atlantic hurricane season set a new record with 27 named hurricanes and tropical storms. Hurricane Katrina devastated New Orleans in August 2005. It was one of the costliest and deadliest storms ever to hit the United States.

Global warming is a serious issue, but we can find solutions for our environmental problems.

For example, for many years, gases called chlorofluorocarbons, or CFCs, were used as coolants in freezers and air conditioners.

By the 1980s, scientists had discovered that CFCs were thinning the ozone layer high in the earth's atmosphere.

THINNING OZONE LAYER

Because the ozone layer helps block the sun's harmful ultraviolet rays, people worked together to protect it.

By the 1990s, many countries had agreed to stop using CFCs. Scientists expect the ozone layer to recover around 2065.

# MORE ABOUT GLOBAL WARMING

Venus is the hottest planet in our solar system. Many astronomers believe its heat is due to a massive greenhouse effect. Carbon dioxide makes up a whopping 97 percent of Venus's atmosphere. The planet's thick clouds and dense atmosphere help trap the sun's heat, making Venus's surface temperature 870 degrees Fahrenheit (466 degrees Celsius). That's hot enough to melt lead!

After carbon dioxide, methane is the greenhouse gas most produced by humans. Methane is released by landfills and is a by-product of coal mining. Believe it or not, cows are also a source of methane. When cows burp or pass gas, they release methane. As the demand for beef rises, more cattle are raised and more methane is released into the air.

The United States is responsible for more greenhouse gas pollution than any other country in the world.

Hurricanes have different names depending on where they occur in the world. If they appear on the Pacific Ocean, they're called typhoons. When they form on the Indian Ocean, they're called tropical cyclones.

Ozone gas can be good or bad, depending on where it lies in the atmosphere. The ozone layer 10 to 30 miles (16 to 48 kilometers) high works as a shield to protect life on earth from the sun's dangerous ultraviolet radiation. This radiation can lead to skin cancer in humans. Nearer the earth's surface, ground-level ozone is a health hazard, damaging lungs and hurting plants.

The Arctic's sea ice is also melting quickly. Because snow and ice are white, the sea ice works like a big mirror, reflecting most of the sun's rays. As global temperatures rise, however, some of the ice melts. This melting reveals the ocean water below. Because the water is darker than the ice, it absorbs more of the sun's energy and warms up. The warmer water leads to even more of the sea ice melting, which leads to even more water being revealed. The cycle goes on and on.

 You've probably seen hybrid cars on the road or on TV. Maybe your family even has one. Hybrid cars run on both gasoline and electricity. Because they don't use as much gas as regular cars, they produce less pollution.

## MORE ABOUT

**SUPER SCIENTIST**

**Real name:** Maxwell J. Axiom
**Hometown:** Seattle, Washington
**Height:** 6' 1"  **Weight:** 192 lbs
**Eyes:** Brown  **Hair:** None

**Super capabilities:** Super intelligence; able to shrink to the size of an atom; sunglasses give x-ray vision; lab coat allows for travel through time and space.

**Origin:** Since birth, Max Axiom seemed destined for greatness. His mother, a marine biologist, taught her son about the mysteries of the sea. His father, a nuclear physicist and volunteer park ranger, schooled Max on the wonders of earth and sky.

One day on a wilderness hike, a megacharged lightning bolt struck Max with blinding fury. When he awoke, Max discovered a newfound energy and set out to learn as much about science as possible. He traveled the globe earning degrees in every aspect of the field. Upon his return, he was ready to share his knowledge and new identity with the world. He had become Max Axiom, Super Scientist.

# GLOSSARY

atmosphere (AT-muhs-fihr)—the mixture of gases that surrounds the earth

average (AV-uh-rij)—a common amount of something; an average amount is found by adding figures together and dividing by the number of figures.

carbon dioxide (KAHR-buhn dye-AHK-side)—a colorless, odorless gas that people and animals breathe out; plants take in carbon dioxide because they need it to live.

climate (KLEYE-mit)—the usual weather that occurs in a place

drought (DROUT)—a long period of weather with little or no rainfall

fossil fuels (FOSS-uhl FYOO-uhls)—natural fuels formed from the remains of plants and animals; coal, oil, and natural gas are fossil fuels.

glacier (GLAY-shur)—a huge moving body of ice found in mountain valleys or polar regions

habitat (HAB-uh-tat)—the natural place and conditions in which a plant or animal lives

ozone layer (OH-zohn LAY-ur)—the thin layer of ozone high above the earth's surface that blocks out some of the sun's harmful rays

photosynthesis (foh-toh-SIN-thuh-sis)—the process by which plant cells use energy from the sun to combine carbon dioxide, water, and minerals to make food for plant growth; photosynthesis releases oxygen into the atmosphere.

radiate (RAY-dee-ate)—to give off energy

**READ MORE**

Cheel, Richard. *Global Warming Alert!* Disaster Alert! New York: Crabtree, 2007.

Farrar, Amy. *Global Warming.* Essential Viewpoints. Edina, Minn.: ABDO, 2008.

Kowalski, Kathiann M. *Global Warming.* Open for Debate. New York: Benchmark Books, 2004.

Morgan, Sally. *From Windmills to Hydrogen Fuel Cells: Discovering Alternative Energy.* Chain Reactions. Chicago: Heinemann, 2007.

Morris, Neil. *Global Warming.* What If We Do Nothing? Milwaukee: World Almanac Library, 2007.

**INTERNET SITES**

FactHound offers a safe, fun way to find Internet sites related to this book. All of the sites on FactHound have been researched by our staff.

Here's how:
1. Visit *www.facthound.com*
2. Choose your grade level.
3. Type in this book ID **1429601396** for age-appropriate sites. You may also browse subjects by clicking on letters, or by clicking on pictures and words.
4. Click on the **Fetch It** button.

**FactHound will fetch the best sites for you!**

# INDEX

## GRAPHIC SCIENCE

### UNDERSTANDING

# GLOBAL WARMING

### with MAX AXIOM
#### SUPER SCIENTIST

by Agnieszka Biskup

illustrated by Cynthia Martin and Bill Anderson

Consultant:
Joseph M. Moran, PhD
Associate Director, Education Program
American Meteorological Society, Washington, D.C.

Graphic Library is published by Capstone Press,
1710 Roe Crest Drive, North Mankato, Minnesota 56003.
www.capstonepub.com

*Library of Congress Cataloging-in-Publication Data*
Biskup, Agnieszka.
    Understanding global warming with Max Axiom, super scientist / by Agnieszka Biskup;
illustrated by Cynthia Martin and Bill Anderson.
    p. cm.—(Graphic library. Graphic science)
    Summary: "In graphic novel format, follows the adventures of Max Axiom as he
explains the science behind global warming"—Provided by publisher.
    Includes bibliographical references and index.
    ISBN-13: 978-1-4296-0139-9 (hardcover)        ISBN-10: 1-4296-0139-6 (hardcover)
    ISBN-13: 978-1-4296-1767-3 (softcover pbk.)   ISBN-10: 1-4296-1767-5 (softcover pbk.)
    1. Global warming—Juvenile literature. 2. Adventure stories—Juvenile literature. I.
Martin, Cynthia, 1961– ill. II. Anderson, Bill, 1963– ill. III. Title. IV. Series.
QC981.8.G56B525 2008
363.738'74—dc22                                                              2007002269

*Art Director and Designer*
Bob Lentz

*Cover Artist*
Tod Smith

*Colorist*
Krista Ward

*Editor*